ALIVE
AND
PARANOID

Published by *Iskra Books* 2024
All rights reserved

RED POETRY COLLECTION

ISKRA BOOKS
US | UK | IRELAND
WWW.ISKRABOOKS.ORG

Iskra Books is an independent scholarly publisher—publishing original
works of revolutionary theory, history, natural science, poetry,
and art, as well as edited collections, new translations, and critical
republications of older works.

ISBN-13: 978-1-0880-2567-3 (*Softcover*)

British Library Cataloguing in Publication Data
A catalogue record for this book is available from the British Library

Library of Congress Cataloging-in-Publication Data
A catalog record for this book is available from the Library of Congress

Cover Design and Typesetting by Ben Stahnke
Interior Photography by D. Musa Springer

D. Musa Springer

ALIVE
AND
PARANOID

I felt bad for the next three or four years, to tell the truth, and those were the years when I wrote most of my poetry. (For my best poems were all written when I felt the worst. When I was happy, I didn't write anything.)

—LANGSTON HUGHES, "THE BIG SEA"

contents

ONE

THIS BOOK WAS WRITTEN IN THE HAMSTER WHEEL, in the sense that D. Musa Springer penned these poems not in leisure but in labor—in spite and because of the sleepless hustle Amerika demands. Such hustle—against the backdrop of a racist, capitalist society—was only survivable because of the poet's own impulse for writing verse. And such an impulse imprisons many poets, consumes them, forcing them to write on the bus to or from work, against the harsh blue light of a smartphone, in the breakroom of an office or a fast food chain, or against the ticking, unforgiving clock.

When poetry is written for survival, not luxury, it is not conventionally marketable: Springer will not be invited to orate at anyone's inauguration and only after these poems are defanged and decontextualized will they be advertised on MARTA's subway cars, if ever. Still, even fresh-off-the-press, this book, with its ruffled feathers and tall, wild grass, offers weaponry and wisdom; insight into the material conditions that forces poetry (as an act of unabridged honesty, as an act of refusal) to be born. This isn't to say that a line from a poem can replace bread or shelter, of course, but to assert the importance of such a refusal in the face of political and cultural hegemony. A hegemony that, in today's world, shapeshifts and can look a lot like... us.

"Counterinsurgencies," Springer tells me on the phone, "the co-optation of our movement," was what compelled them to publish this book of poems. "Celebrities making millions of dollars off of Black death." The materiality of *Alive and Paranoid* is what makes it so vital, especially in a literary economy when much of the poetry on the shelves is theater and performance; when much of the "revolutionary" and "anti-racist" poetry recognized by the literary world was written on expensive couches, in expensive houses, in oblivion.

Springer's "poetry of purpose," is personal and incendiary, it gloats and it weeps, and, most importantly, it is not neatly-trimmed to fit within the borders of a sparkly billboard screen in Times Square. It is blunt and unconcerned with platitudes. *Alive and Paranoid* journeys through Atlanta, Cuba, dreamscapes of Palestine, and the sonic values of hip-hop, offering a kaleidoscopic look, even a sense of liberty, into Springer's life IN THE HAMSTER WHEEL.

—MOHAMMED EL-KURD
JERUSALEM, OCCUPIED PALESTINE

TWO

I T'S TRUE. And nobody wants to say it, but we artists take ourselves far too seriously. This is not an unfounded criticism, because the call is definitely coming from inside the house. It's the result of the various contradictions that all of us must contend with under neoliberal capitalism. It's not that artists, poets specifically, across time have not had to battle with misplaced ego, main character syndrome, and intense savior complexes (because they certainly did). It's more that the specific economic and political orientation of our time (neoliberalism) drives us toward monetizing every single aspect of our lives, including our identities and our art. In the United States today, there is no shortage of "Black and proud" literary works; they are literally pouring off of the displays and shelves in your local bookstore.

Someone no less the wiser could look at this moment on the surface and call it a new "Renaissance" of sorts, invoking the histories of people like Langston Hughes, or figures of the Black Arts Movement like Gwendolyn Brooks and Amiri Baraka. But this is a deception. We have lied to ourselves for much too long. Somewhere along the journey toward "diversity," "representation," and "inclusion" we forgot that we were at war with capitalism, with imperialism, with ourselves.

And so the art we put out to the world is beautiful! It's dark skin greased up under blue lights. Neat cornrows braided defiantly from hairline to neck. It's kente. It's diasporic, complete with the obligatory mentions of the mango tree in the neighbor's yard of days past. It's creative. It's sassy. It has a degree from Spelman, or Morehouse, or Howard. It's so Black and proud, and it's become borderline counter-revolutionary.

So, what is the role of the Black artist? And is it even fair to ask such a question? "All is fair in love and war." Our friendship only knows one way to make it out alive: organize, organize, organize.

For us, *Alive and Paranoid* is more than the artistic ramblings of a friend. It is hours and hours of ki kis, criticisms, and disagreements passed back and forth on Whatsapp and in person. In these pages, you will find many reflections that Musa wrote live and direct from Havana, Cuba, where people have been struggling under the weight of 60-year-old economic sanctions placed on the country—with the intent to kill.

Musa wrote these poems while there in solidarity with family they have built on the island over the past decade as an anti-sanctions organizer. On many of those trips, they arrived with less than 12 USD in their bank account. We know this because we are the ones who had to check for them (because US banks are inaccessible from Cuba.)

You will read about settler colonialism and solidarity with Palestine. You will read about Atlanta, a neo-colonial nightmare built on top of the bones of Indigenous peoples and the muffled cries of a forgotten African nation.

Just as it is intimate for Musa to release these words to the world, we feel we are also inviting you to read, through our eyes, how we have watched our homie take on mental illness, faith, love, and media corporations out to steal their labor and their light. How we have watched Musa wage war on their own memory in order to forget things too expensive to remember, and remember things too expensive to forget. Sometimes this nigga is writin', sometimes this nigga is rappin', sometimes this nigga is preaching, and sometimes it's all the same.

If it is true that the best art is made from just living life, we hope that you will enjoy this art born out of the fight to birth one worth living!

—ERICA + SALIFU

these pages **are** not **special**

i, the poet, am not special,
nor are the words, emotions,
and experiences expressed here.

written between bouts of bitterness, political misery, paranoia,
mania, compulsions, protest,
and the dismal adventures of coming to grips with the fucking
uselessness of my own ambitions,
this is a book of thoughts as clear and concise as i could possibly
make them,
and nothing is special about any of it.

nothing particularly new is held in this collection of cold pressed
sensation.
my pen documents waves of grieving responses to the burning
world.
nothing more, nothing less.

truth terrified me into writing many of these diatribes, and in truth
there is a warmth
which at times heals, other times burns, and in any case is not so
special.
we must fight the urge to make the truth seem special.
we do not have to exceptionalize the truth, an experience, nor an
emotion to honor it
and we must fight the push to do so and call it poetry.

the only place where my thoughts make sense anymore is inside
poems,
where i am able to express my self however i need to
where my sentences may flow without intrusive hurdles,

compulsive doubt, stammering guilt, or stuttering memory,
and a brake pad slamming "i forgot what i waz about to say"
is nothing more than a break in a single line of poetry.

what is special, however, is that you, dear reader,
may find yourself reflected within some of the lines;
mirrors hiding among the stanzas may ask your forgiveness,
and daggers lying along the way may remove themselves from your
path.

this small stack is an open flesh wound of a ~~boy~~
navigating a world endlessly against ~~him~~
well acquainted with death but never inviting it for dinner
exploring what it means to live within hell
knowing heaven is around the corner with patience
obsessing over that which cannot be changed alone
dying to know the meaning of rebirth
struggling to string together a sentence or two
unable to see or breath through thick anxious clouds
still somehow maneuvering as if stillness is not an option
and planting seeds at every turn desperately trying to regrow sanity.

this book is nothing but whispers which i have already given to the
Earth
forged through THE CREATOR, righteously burdened by my ancestor's
air.
is nothing, this book. you is you, and i is i, and none of us is THE
MOST HIGH.

(inside these curved walls i speak to YOU)

1

The ~~poem~~ Art was a dream that was
and tired of being inside of an Amerika
up and make music and be mad and be
 and bleed and hide his tears and love his
and dress like he's in a hip-hop video
Shoved him how to plant a garden and
to kill himself or how not to hate how
or how not to feel alone ~~and~~ worthless whe
to burn everything down when the rage start~~s~~. H
one pulling the trigger. The anger consumed him be
teach him to teach himself how to be himself
he drowned a few times because no one ever
the water and he kept saying he wouldn't a
was never too sure what box to put him in. So
told him to work hard to get to the top but
hurt and feet got sore and eyes grew dry and
the gold at the top of the pyramid. Dad didn't
real the full ~~poem~~ when ~~t~~he gave ~~it~~ th
Smelled like lemon pepper wings and a 40 a
about crashing into a tree every time he
~~Poem~~ Art feels much more like a letter o
was writing and talking to Allah
if it was, his hands or his heart th
to ~~make~~ free the poem stuck in his head o

a grayish-black boy who was frustrated
asking him to be still and quiet and look
not be too queer and pray 5 times a day
speak english and turn his music down
s diary a journal But they never
ine. They never learned him how not to want
got caught in his hair when he played w/it
ne likes pass on him for white guys or how nt
d believing in God long enough to realize she was the
nted the world to teach him to day-dream and
air and be his nail polish and lick his tears and
eet in the water to show him how to stay above
in but capitalism had other plans. The world
him at the bottom of a pyramid scheme and it
how much his grayish-black hands bled and head
nd dick got tired and spine broke he was never
sens and Mom said she did but never even
so eventually the poem became a dream that
ers side of a '96 Honda Civic that he thought
highway to head to the **masjid** and this
for help or a prayer but he thought he
was you who kept answering me He asked
him hurt so bad and what he could do
tired of waiting for the world to respond and

the ~~poem~~ art was a dream that was inside of a grayish-black ~~boy~~ who was frustrated and tired of being inside of an Amerika that kept asking ~~him~~ to be still and quiet and look up and make music and be mad and be closed and not be too queer and pray 5 times a day and bleed and hide ~~his~~ tears and love ~~his~~ kountry and speak english and turn ~~his~~ music down and dress like ~~he's~~ in a hip-hop video and call ~~his~~ diary a journal but they never showed ~~him~~ how to plant a garden and keep it alive. they never learned ~~him~~ how not to want to kill ~~himself~~ or how not to hate how ~~his~~ fingers got caught in ~~his~~ hair when ~~he~~ played with it or how not to feel alone and worthless when the guys ~~he~~ likes pass on ~~him~~ for white guys or how not to burn everything down when the rage starts. ~~he~~ only stopped believing in God long enough to realize she was the one pulling the trigger. the anger consumed ~~him~~ because ~~he~~ wanted the world to teach ~~him~~ how to day-dream and teach ~~him~~ how to teach ~~himself~~ to be ~~himself~~ and be ~~his~~ hair and be ~~his~~ nail polish and lick ~~his~~ tears and ~~he~~ drowned a few times because no one ever dipped ~~his~~ feet in the water to show ~~him~~ how to stay above the water and ~~he~~ kept saying ~~he~~ wouldn't drown again but capitalism had other plans. the world was never too sure what box to put ~~him~~ in so it just put ~~him~~ at the bottom of a pyramid scheme and it told ~~him~~ to work hard to get to the top but no matter how hard ~~his~~ grayish-black hand bled and head hurt and feet got sore and eyes grew dry and nose bled and dick got tired and spine broke ~~he~~ was never the gold at the top of the pyramid. dad didn't like ~~his poem~~ art and ~~dad~~ mom said she did but never even read the full ~~poem~~ art when ~~I~~ ~~he~~ gave them to her. so eventually the poem became a dream that smelled like lemon pepper wings and a 40oz and the driver's side of a '96 Honda Civic that ~~he~~ thought about crashing into a tree every time ~~he~~ got on the highway to head to the masjid and this ~~poem~~ art feels much more like a letter or a call for help or a prayer but ~~he~~ thought ~~he~~ was writing and talking to Allah but it was (you) who kept answering. ~~he~~ asked if it was ~~his~~ hands or

his heart that made him hurt so bad and what he could do to free
the poem stuck in his head and he got tired of waiting for the world
to respond and

I'D RATHER BE

ALIVE AND PARANOID

THAN DEAD AND RIGHT.

workkk

oatmeal in my bowl

        work

tea in my cup

           work

turn the lights on

     work

heat in my vents

       work

gotta feed the cat

   work

open up the laptop

          work

~~pay all my taxes~~

      work

take my medicine

            work

gas in the car

       work

condoms and lube

     work

work

       work

water in my faucets

   work

head on a pillow

      work

work

       work

asthma inhaler

   work

food in my belly
                                        work
talk on the phone
                  work
water the plants
                       work
more medicine
                    work

                                                  work
glasses for the nighttime
                              work
a fresh retwist
throw in a fresh fade
                  work
no movie theater
                                  work
gotta pay the barber
                                              work
low on groceries
                        work
gotta doctor's visit
necesito pay the plug
                  w   or   k
                              work
y necesito pay rent
                                            work
want some new books
                        work
but need clothes on my back

work

blanket on my bed
     work

health insurance
    work

a little therapy
    work   work
        work
    work   work   work

new paint brushes
               work

oop an asthma attack
                 work

i wanted concealer
    werk

nother death a nother death
   work work work workkrowkrowkkrowkroworkkwworkwork-
               krowworkkkroworkwork

a manic episode
        work

and a panic attack
      wor k   work

need some new headphones
        work

iwork usedwork towork cutwork mywork legswork work
        andwork nowwork iwork havework
              work
    intrusivework throughtswork aboutwork itwork
work   work workworkkwork workworkk krowwork

                    work
pain in my chest
                              work
lotsa student loans
                                        work
ache behind my left eye
                                              work
dinner every night
                                                    work
lexapro, workworkwork work lamictal, work
                              w   o   r   k
mirtazapine   w   w
                    ork   ork
all this debt
                                                    work
justa lil bit of weed
                                              wo   rk
a lil bit o life
                                              w   ork
and a whole lotta deathwork work workkrowworkkrow work
                                        work
coffin
                              work
funeral
                              work

shadow, or reason x i don't be online **as much** anymore

the grey cat—russian blue, eyes green—
with a baker's dozen different nicknames
on a good week / who makes cameos
in computer screens a little too often /
whose affection is but an act of faith /
don't give a shit about a blue bubble
or a green one and don't play social
media games / can't use an iphone
android / nor name a brand aloud
and don't care to learn how to
properly use a laptop or
check a bank account
on her watch while
talking to A.I.
about dinner or
about money or
about the weather
or her packed schedule,
but she somehow knows
that when little baby cousin
crawls towards the staircase
on his wobbly play-doh knees
she needs to get his attention
and get him away from there fast /
she knows how to pop baby's hands
when he reaches for the balcony railing
and she didn't need a ~~google~~_search or
an infectious teek tawk tutorial to learn it
nor did she need the good deed to be seen
by a digital audience tapping their approval.

first **class**

---

the sweat
from nervous jitters
will salt the skin.
charger cords
to tie that ham hock thigh
right on up—
pass the Muthufukin pepper!
i'm cookin over here!

i walk by and see dinner
scrolling on an ipad
making sure not to
catch any eye contact.
they know their crimes
or some other blood
got them in that seat.

they know deep down one day we'll call that bluff
we'll baste their asses with travel size wine bottles,
keep silver cutlery on us and always a sharp knife
to use when the peanuts and pretzels ain't enough.

the **end** of the fucking world came

again in May [that] year.

nine minutes and twenty-nine seconds

stretched to hours, broke to days, forced into months.

it sounded the same way the end of the world always sounds

it looked the same way the end of the world has always looked

for a moment it felt like the end of the world is supposed to feel

the pessimists missed it again, not knowing that

the end of the world looks like fire and steel and muscle,

not tenured talk and panels and academic immunity and nihilism.

and the optimists and the humanists missed it too, the end of the world,

spending too much time and energy and magic

trying to convince evil of itself, trying to convince evil of goodness,

trying to convince the prison wardens of the power of love,

trying to convince the prison guards of the power of the vote,

trying to convince prisoners of the power of patience

instead of telling patience to move the fuck out of the way.

others puffed themselves into obscurity, drank themselves anxious,

fucked themselves numb, prayed themselves away from the view of the fire.

some scribbled books about "looting" and "primitive accumulation"

and transubstantiation and race and transmogrification

and criticism and critique of the criticism and

responses to the critique of the criticism

for jobs in the criticism industrial complex

and hefty checks from the conversation industrial complex.

others thinkpiece'd the end of the world into a million pieces

filling pages of internet with Black death,

while some were busy pouring tear gas solution

in our siblings' eyes and passing community inhalers

through thick tearful gas clouds and lost eyesight from rubber bullets

and forgot the ability to tell if the blood on their chin was from

a pig's baton or if they coughed it up or if it didn't belong to them at all

or if it got onto them when they were kettled and snatched up

in the crowd while running back to base to re-organize.

i knew it was the end of the fucking world when we heard more from

those that spoke about bricks but never built a home, never threw one,

who talked about r/evolution but never held a gun or a hand,

who never had to rob peter to pay paul or set fires to feel warmth,

than those who know what it means to look a cub in the eye and shout "alhamdulilah!"

because you know it will one day become a lion, or a panther,

and that this beast could very well bite off your hand too

if you aren't ready and careful.

when everywhere we turned freedom dreams were all we heard

and silence befell those who had already seen the world end a few times

and suffered because of it, i knew it was time for

the end of the fucking world[1]

1   First published in *Hood Communist*, 2021.

rivers & the **sea**

when he passed over the mighty Mississippi,
he realized the ancestors' rivers he knew:
the Congo, the Nile, the Niger Delta,
and a few more, said Langston Hughes.

i read his words one scorching Matanzas day
on a locals beach full of natural hair,
surrounded by strangers, friends from far away,
and a revolutionary smell filling the air.

no tourists in sight, and i blend in.
they spit rum as offering for the orishas,
thank the taxi driver with cigarette grins,
and invite me to play ball in the sand.

in Africa, Hughes says, he wasn't Black,
wasn't white neither, and wasn't African.
they didn't know what to do with him
and he ain't know how to feel about it.

on *Playa El Tenis* they don't know
what to do with me neither:
honorary member of revolutions ago,
anemic guest returning with fever.

pale on the outside, dark in the heart,
one cuban says to me passing the lighter.
i could never say that in the states,
but he indeed saw an african heart.

deep waves whisper stories of the ages:
love interrupted, jumping ships in tears,
and through the ebb and flow of time,
i'm tethered to my forebears here.

if Hughes saw rivers of ancestors past,
then i sit here writing as i witness the sea.
in all its glory, i come to know the waters
and how they stole something from me.[2]

2   First published in *Hood Communist*, 2023.

(sickle specters:
what's mine is ours,
and what's yours is ours,
and what's ours is everyone's,

only if we acknowledge
what's theirs is ours,
and really mean it
when we say it,
and then do
something
bout it.)

and this city is a fiery **grave**

Atlanta showed me my first pig carriage in flames.
I am learning how to pour gasoline on discourse.
—MOHAMMED EL-KURD

atlanta taught me a poem's a dead man walking, that wordy flesh is already dead by the time it hits your hands. atlanta taught me what it iz, what it ain't, and what it's gon' be: chalky hands tie tight strings at the ribcages, through ankles and fingertips, just behind the neck up through the forehead, and with puppetmaster precision sit back and enjoy the show. glass all under my eyelids from staring at storms through the window. glass under my gums from them days chewing on history. atlanta pulled up its shirt and showed me a bruise shaped like a grave. atlanta peeled back its skin, sat me down, crunched the numbers, explained that child murders have turned a profit since '79, and '79 before that, and '79 before that, and so why would they stop grinding the bones now? i didn't know a death more intimate than witnessing a chamelion impaled mid color change. some called it a tragedy, others called it casual and made dua in lemon pepper wet. there's stammered memory in the water here. atlanta taught me to teach my damn self. taught me to sell a dream, steal a hope, and buy a buck. that angels got good aim, too. this city eats its martyrs, celebrates when they let go of its teeth. it teaches its young to fake life and hide all that dead in their eyes if they want to survive. that highways are rest stops for crowds of protested bones. that a city can be a company's personality trait. that an acquaintance is an acquaintance, and you ain't no friend until you're dead. i place the microphone to the grave and chuckle. the crowd uncontrollable as it laughs and bobs its head through another death called tuesday blues. the dirt has seen this all before, the laughter masking tears, and asks if we've seen the gas prices.

(chewed on too many rose thorns
smelled too much tear gas
felt too many winters this year

without an umbrella for too many storms
sat passenger seat for too many crashes
gave more than i received in return this year

got handfuls of busted lips and gnashed my teef away
wondered about the thousands of different ways
tonight's daft poem could have turned out

(words used to build the mountains
i'd climb up and now they dig
trenches i fear i cannot escape)

dreamed too close to the sun
melted into ashes in the wind
missed too many jummahs this year

gripped skin scrawled with calamity
lashed out at life more than death
trudged in useless trauma this year

and still, all i know is all that i am:
nothing but a pebble drowned
beneath life, gazing upwards.

a deep, rolling sigh
creeping down the side
of the glass on a hot day.)

and we will dare to slay
these malevolent giants—
downright dastardly dragons—

if perhaps for nothing more

than to swing like children
in the charred rubble
of their decaying ribcages

verzuz, or the interconnectedness of that **politician** popping up on yo screen

the kkklinton empire shouted 'super predator'
into the weather that gave me fucking asthma
and rained down a baby jail state psychiatric hospital
immigrant detention center border detention facility
in school suspension room holding cell
metal detector and black site in every hood,

that same short heel pant suit wearin woman
that authorized child soldiers in southern sudan
called amerika the midwife of that country's birth
before arming all sides and slapping it on the ass with
sanctions,
whose foundation made millions in haiti made millions in
amerikkka
made millions off families having to pay jpay for phonecalls
and emails
who made millions off the amerikan brutality wrought onto
Qaddafi,

i'm supposed to care what the fuck they have to say?
i'm supposed to sip earl grey and crunch kale wraps
while they play political marionettes with my nerves?

i'm expected to peacefully pet puppies in the park
while they pour gasoline in my shoes like a jaded ex?

one way or another their signatures make it to
the prison cells that encage black children
put black blood in white bank accounts
pays apocalypse a christmas bonus
keep police on the streets
paid by the same signatures
that draft weapons deals that launch
the same tear gas in Palestine in Atlanta
the same milky terror found in Haiti in Harlem,

backed by the same capitalists building buildings
on uneven trade and colonized fundations
with support from billion dollar nonprofits
and million dollar celebrities
who tell us to vote blue
even though we're
seeing red,

and we're supposed to care what the fuck they have to say?
we're supposed to wait with coupons in the self-checkout line
while they use bloodied banks to buy the building next door?
we're expected to play pattycake in a wintery voting booth
while they calculate the cost of counting the dead this time?
while they put a price tag on a lung, a headshot, and a retweet?

they trade their deeds in leashed rappers, not dollars,

profiting from billion dollar social media corporations

profiting from billion dollar streaming corporations

profiting from trillion dollar technology corporations

profiting from million dollar sweatshop clothing brands

profiting from capitalist empires profiting from imperialism

profiting from gentrification profiting from prisons profiting from,

me

sitting on my damn phone livestreaming the event,

(something... something... election...

but this time kkklinton's in blackface[3])

while they tell us about the power of a vote and the evil of a riot

before the blood on the sidewalk even dried,

before their next single dropped and the checks cleared

before wakanda and lion king hit streaming services

before the fires stopped before the blue vest popped

before the feds rolled up at our doors,

we're supposed to care what the fuck these people have to say?

---

3   Refers to Stacey Abrams appearing on a Verzuz battle in 2020, in the midst of uprisings, to tell folks to vote blue. This poem was written that same night.

65 years, **give** or take

the flight always a family affair,
cigarette hands and coffee breath
smelling up and down the aisles.

figures in tight handmedowns traipse,
speak as lively as their clothes colorful.
you'd think they weren't strangers.

we traverse unblocked seas,
waves older than any empire
worshipping Yemayá from below.

no landing is without a round of applause—
for the wheels to touch down here
is to again loudly defy death.

i look out my window with anticipation,
unable to ever forget that every arrival
is to escape momentarily capitalism's clasp.

here, *chisme* is a currency
worth more than pesos:
some call it revolutionary vigilance.

some barely whisper about the death in their rice,
while their neighbors have too much to say about it.
others don't know who to be mad at, but mad they are.

the trash is piling up on Enfanta again—
no hay combustible, no hay garbage trucks.
billboards everywhere denounce the blockade.

many sell *maní* from their front doors
because it's sweeter than anything else
the island has to offer them right now.

the pizzas have a bit less cheese and sauce every time,
but still i walk along Neptuno each day for lunch
to devour one on the sidewalk under the hot sun.

warriors in an unwanted dance,
they just want a little milk, shoes that fit,
coffee, ibuprofen, eyeglasses—sovereignty.

Maritza's smile reminds me that for 65 years give or take
these people have all gnawed on death's bones
and washed it all down with life for breakfast.

(stare
in
the
eyes
of
your truth:
i
hope
it
don't
nightmare
you)

*[...] we're like a **family** here

and they always say it without
realizing how much they admit
in that stupid little sentence.

like family won't fuck up your mental
snatch the food right outta your fridge
and leave you sleeping cold in a '96 honda.

like family ain't capable of fuckin you up
to the point you never wanna see they face again.
like a cousin never made your stomach turn.

like half the planet ain't running around right now
mad at the world mad at the mirror mad at they daddies
mad as hell at their families and takin it out on all us.

like we don't all got an uncle or two
with a jaw we still wanna rock one good time
for that dumb shit he said years ago.

how insidious it is that my paycheck is
what diamonds are to a snake's eyes
or a jewel thief or a colonizer on the continent

or a marketing team
to their consumption addicts
or to them crackers snappin the whip.

and they have the cauliflower audacity
to look me direct in my baggy ass eyes
and really feel it deep down when they say [...]*

i don't believe in hell but i do believe in fire

(and i believe in my desire to never touch it again)
and i believe in heaven but i've been told
it doesn't believe in me (some shit about sin)

and i believe in praying five times a day but
i know that on certain days half those prayers
are asking what They meant in surah al-baqarah
when They said He's always with those who are patient

because sometimes patience is a liberal muthufucka
you've got to pick up and move out the fuckin way
and other times patience is compromise is death
is a smiling politician you gotta mow right on over

is a boss you gotta chump off on the sales floor
is a dangerous seat at the table in a house of ashes
is salt in a bleeding throat is being quiet and polite
while they take forks and eat away at your flesh

is whoever them muthufuckers are that put biden-harris-
(hillary-obama-cortez-omar-pelosi-abrams-sanders-buttigieg)
campaign signs over the faces of black people killed by kkkops
on the wall outside the white house where revolution didn't
happen.

is i lost you yesterday, is i lost myself today
is i lost patience, is i lost self is i lost my cool is i lost my
fuckin job
is i lost the batteries to my sanity/ lost the code to the safe

lost sleep
lost my wallet lost my watch lost my camera and my phone
lost a lot to the fire/ lost my way lost my hope and my filter
lost you, lost my desire to crawl back into myself
and smile at broken mirrors/ lost you yesterday lost the war
lost my muthufuckin train of thought and marbles

(but i damn sure won't lose or admit defeat to an empire
that has lost to guerilla fighters in jungles, embarrassed
by free breakfast programs and black book stores)

is a kkkingdom of krooks that lose every single night
as the sun sets on a free matanzas,
sending jokes in gq suits to fail in caracas,
whose name conjures burning flags, guttural spits
in tehran, in beirut, in ramallah, in pyongyang,
in atlanta, in port-au-prince, in accra, in kingston, in every
prison.

i don't believe in hell but if one exists then surely
       it's full of them patient muthufuckas
       preaching peace in the face of fire
       poisoned water stolen land a melting earth
       drone strikes sanctions and asthma attacks

a southern sky weeps with passion
as it comes to know
its child:

her red clay
birthed brown
umber beauty.

all the leaves
whisper histories
of softened summers
and sweet springs
and palms

now calloused
with coffee bean hands
and wedding rings.

my father,
a beer of love and laughter
poured into a falcons jersey.

wide smiles
burst from him,
stored, patiently awaiting
debut since childhood.

a welder,
works with fire.
a child,
whose father

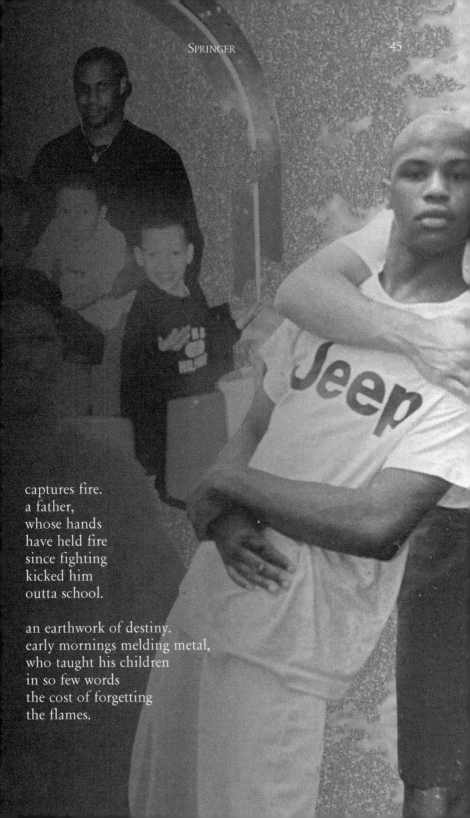

captures fire.
a father,
whose hands
have held fire
since fighting
kicked him
outta school.

an earthwork of destiny.
early mornings melding metal,
who taught his children
in so few words
the cost of forgetting
the flames.

(this one's

    for DeShawn.

        and Monte.

            and Kiwan.

                and DeLa.

                    and Nico.

                        and Keith.

and M******. i still call your old phone number sometimes, just to hear you on the voicemail.

i don't leave messages often, because i fear the day it says "this mailbox is full, goodbye,"

and i know it will feel too much like another endless departure from you.

but when i do speak to you, i weep love. my tears miss you, and i pray they fall into the ocean

and the ancestors deliver them to you. i pray. i pray. i pray. i pray. i pray.

i drive by your home sometimes and laugh at how terrified i
was of the barking cocker spaniel in your garage. your mother's
soul embraces me from the driveway and i still feel her every
grief from years away. i remember where you taught me to play
basketball, how we'd cross through backyards and over fences
and run from the rottweilers just to get to our special hiding
spot.

the kisses on my neck remain soft after these years. i trace that
spot with my fingertips and remember our childish lips explor-
ing each other under the indigo of a summer night. the wind
reminds me of how fresh

your love smelled, and i release my sadness into it again and
again and again.

this one's for you.)

dissertation for dead scholars

No thesis existed for burning cities down at such a rampant rate.
—COURTNEY LOVE

no thesis needed for twistin knives
at such a rampant rate.
no docs and no fucking dissertations
on unaliving pigs in a righteous rage.
no powerpoint presentations for thumbs
only bleeding on the page.
no research fucking committees
for breaking the homies from the cage.

all them freedom dreams
and they still nightmare you.
most likely to let
the alphabet boys
multi-hyphen you.
most likely to let
the rifle boom
frighten you.

i can almost **remember**

that singsong taste, a salty slowdrawl across mytongue
always landing ona perfect lil sweetspot.

shabby two by fo's with deep copperrusted nails
holdin sunbathin watermelons, dark p-cans,
tomatoesandapples, peaches too if wewas lucky,
all existing to be praised by youth. a roadside divinity.
that battered strandboard stained with thick letters
slowly scribbled across with permanent marker:

good god get them bad boys fromthespoon
to that styrofoamcup clothed in brown bag,
get them goobas tootha nearest register
grab a few of 'em georgiapeaches too—
weigh it up. cash only. smiles appreciated,
tips even better.

wet hot pot of shell sucking spicy nutty goodness
sitting in my lap that gush of kongo's nguba
between my teeth a rush of carver's legacy
hitting all the spots smacking loud and then hushed.
joyful goodstuff. gullah godsend sold by the pound
paid in quarters and crumpled dollars, devoured.

you ain't eatin em right, babe
you gottapop the whole thang in your mouf—
like this—

he watches hungered eyes examine the cup
finding the best one / natural instinct
plucking it from its spice bath into my mouf
with the skill of a southern assassin.

put it right there and bite, but not too hard
just enough to break that outershell
justenough to slurp thajuices out
enough ta get to tha meat.
no worries   bout a mess—slurp!

swollen laugher underneath a noisy georgia sky reminds me:
time and distance and my own neglect stole these from me.
he asks, why we don't really see them around anymore?

how does a lil hot boiled peanut compete with capitalism?

gum **budget** (2:195)

cutting it out / yanking it from my throat

with slight hesitation on my end / was the best decision i made /

(like yo parent tying up yo loose tooth to a door /

you trust them / just to slam it shut)

picked my first pinch / against the lips at fourteen

seeds planted by my own fingertips, all dreamt up alongside tattoos

and shady alleys, backstage at *the seven venue* laying my head against

the speakers' vibrations / til it hurt but helped to not feel for the moment /

when escape was an outlet unafforded / those smooth moments between drags

/ felt like peace.

strong roots don't die easy. sometimes killing can be a challenge / and they withstand

neglect better than a paranoid boy / even when you cut the fruits off,

prune the leaves back / chop at the wooded branches /

until you're left with a stump to grind /

and instead of grinding that stump you leave it as a cautionary tail

to stumble over as many times as it takes.

/ and even then, the roots still remain

still grow beneath the skin / scattered veins of brown blood /

sprouting new life through the neglectful winters.

i must devote my substance to ALLAH's path /

resist the desire of my hands to throw me into destruction.

no redemption for the compradors of the self / nor sellouts to the dunya.

my lungs are by design / that i may breathe, by design / that i should do good,

by design /

/ yet i would be a liar to poetry / and a thief to the truth

if i did not admit to myself or god or / Whoever is listening

that not a day breaks without thinking about /

that peace:

/ when i don't see someone with one and feel compelled to join /

where i don't think about it and then want to do it / or feel the roots still lingering in my throat /

egging me on / knowing i'd rather trip over roots every fuckin day / than rip them up.

after a long day at work at Redf**h when i have to chew on a toothpick or a natural unrefined tip curled

up in my mouth / because i miss the oral fixation / the candy

you slosh around with your tongue during lunch break / that you think about for hours.

/when you try to split it with a friend and the guilt / sets in too quick /

you take a deep breath and say *alhamdulillah*, / *i will just stick with my hands*

hovering around my head / *my face* / *all day and this increased chewing gum budge*t

and remember that the knife to cut it out / yanking it from my throat

/ was the best blessing God gave /

and i'm **not** trying

to cheat death
i want to eat it
a full fucking plate—*desayuno*.
i want to look greedy with all the death
stuffed on my spork spilling from my mouth
shoved in my fridge that i'm not sharing
that i'm heating and salting until it
becomes the ocean and drowns me
that i'm grabbing from all around
and stashing in tightly locked vaults
hoarded with passion in cupboards
pantry shelves for my tongue only.

i washed it down drinking misty, shadowy silhouettes
and gargling the fucking desert last time
and i wanna do it all again this time:
pop a handful of doubts
in my mouf for fresh breath just in case
i finally meet face to face again with
THE MOST HIGH, or The Linoleum Floor

when they get **me**

will i be unloading bags from my car
picking up the heavy ones for my partner
laughter and music still spilling from open doors
when they get me?

will i leave blood stains
on the floor of a mosque
or watch the guards laugh
as i beg for my inhaler?

where will it happen?
somewhere they knew i would be
somewhere i knew they would be
somewhere i knew not to fear
somewhere i trusted too much?

would it be a bomb hidden in my mailbox?
a rush into my home? my job?
will it be when i let my guard down,
hit the blunt with my sisters
and bike across the city as if
the world briefly doesn't hate us?
will i know it's coming (will i
feel it?) or will instinct fail me?

will my mother be okay?
will she get an insurance check?
will they mail her
my bloody clothes
like they did Pat Rodney?
are others at risk? could it spread?

if they try but fail,
what next?

will i be forty years
incognegro in camaguey
with my guard down
when they get me?
will i reach forty?

or or or maybe i will be on the frontlines
under the heat of summer clashes
in a blaze of black bloodied glory
the kids who drank spoonfuls of revolution
will speak of for generations to come,
right?

will they catch me on the run?
will they get me in hiding?
will they find me in the safe house
surrounded by steel, gunpowder,
burner phones, a hundred copies
of that pesky little red book
and about a dozen revolutionaries
who didn't know when to give up?
will they drop a drone on us
smack dab in the middle of the
same hood that raised me?

what will they tell the media
to tell the people
to turn them against me?
will they say i stockpiled weapons
or will they say i had *real* bad ideas?
will they get me all alone
wasting away in a prison cell,
eaten alive by bed bugs
and state-sponsored shanks?

how will they justify it?
will they even need to
if they've already got me?

will i be able to get
a few of them first?

head bone (**snuffuhnassi**)

head bone connected to the neck bone connected to the
chest bone connected to the stomach connected to the
hip bones connected to the leg bone connected to the
foot bone connected to the boot bone connected to the
steel toe connected to the pig's face connected to the
pig's bones connected to the steel toe connected to the
pig's face connected to shoe lace connected to the
pig's brain connected to the fascism connected to the
white house connected to the bullets connected to the
concrete connected to the curb connected to the stomp
connected to the stomp connected to the stomp
connected to the stomp connected to the stomp
connected to the stomp connected to the crunch
connected to the blood connected to the steel toe

hair line connected to head bone connected to the
eye brows connected to the skin connected to the
mouf connected to the teef bone connected to the
smile connected to the charm bone connected to the
tan suit connected to the shoulder bone connected to the
torso connected to the arm bone connected to the
wrist bone connected to the layups connected to the
media connected to the paperwork connected to the
pen connected to the signatures connected to the
drone strikes connected to the weddings connected to the
drone strikes connected to the jummahs connected to the
mosques connected to the hospitals connected to the
drone strikes connected to the drone strikes connected to the
homes connected to the lives connected to the
victims connected to the oil connected to the
money connected to the land connected to the

sanctions connected to the fruit connected to

NGOs connected to militias connected to the
lithium connected to the coups connected to the
copper connected to the NED connected to the
cobalt connected to the banks connected to the
coltan connected to the cellphones connected to the
diamonds connected to the loans connected to the
gold connected to bananas connected to the
rum connected to the cigars connected to the
revolution connected to the sanctions connected to the
spies connected to the coups connected to the
power connected to the sanctions connected to the
death connected to the pen connected to the
signatures connected to the cages connected to the
children connected to the border connected to the
drugs connected to the wars connected to the
CIA connected to the layups connected to the
wrist bone connected to the magazines connected to the
photoshoots connected to the drone strikes connected to the
mouf connected to the president connected to the
tan suit connected to celebrity connected to the
liberals connected to republicans connected to the
democrats connected to hegemony connected to the

brain bone connected to the heart bone
connected to the rib bone connected to the
stomp connected to the steel toe connected to the
stomp connected to the stomp connected to the
stomp connected to the stomp connected to the
hips connected to the liver connected to the
genitals connected to the blood connected to the
veins connected to the muscles connected to the
lungs connected to the air connected to the oxygen
connected to the lungs connected to the clouds
connected to the land connected to the landfills
connected to the waste connected to the plastics

connected to the oil connected to the business
connected to the air connected to the water
connected to the faucet connected to the lead
connected to the bladder connected to the stomach
connected to the gut connected to the skin
connected to the eyes connected to the ears
connected to the mind connected to the mind
connected to the mind connected to the news
connected to the capitalists connected to the
wars connected to the drones connected to the
bombs connected to debris connected to the
pain connected to the profit
connected to the landfills connected to the asthma
connected to the cockroaches connected to the asthma
connected to the cancer connected to the deaths
connected to the lives connected to the lies
connected to the market connected to the map
connected to the world connected to the empire
connected to the colony connected to the plantation
connected to enslavement connected to—

title **lodged** in between a coherent thought's teef

we are not the same / you ain't messin' with my intellect / so your best bet / is just to keep it on the internet
—CAKES DA KILLA, "DON DADA"

1.
met a sheeta paper down at parchman
who told me all about the time
he got crinkled up real nice
and thrown in the bin.

2.
when you try too hard to connect all the dots
you end up looking like you were the target
in an unwanted game of dive bar darts.

3.
everybody forgets they ain't learn
that alberta got shot too
in that same church pew
where she directed the choir til '92:
her name wasn't martin
and neither is you.

4.
you been coughing diff-rent
ever since the tear gas that summer
and good luck on tryna get a check from that:
kinda fucked up isn't it?
your work speaks for itself

if you gotta stay quiet for a bit.

5.
they waited til ramadan began
to really throw it all at you.
played their strongest hand
and really thought you'd fold:
little did them weak duds know
they went low but you stay lower
you take shots like a vested bolder
and stay on the line with the most high
fast with folks who fought battles so colder.

5.1
you met the creator ina waffle house bathroom
they asked for your repentance in blood or sweat:
you were too scarred to break iftar's neck
and too scared to storm to your tomb.

5.2
in the parking lot life and death
and every thing in between
took greedy bites out your liver
put some in pockets to save for later
slurped on your femur something mean
just to spit you out like a dozen spoiled wings.
how the fuck did you get caught up in the gunfight
are you allowed to ask around is the feds in sight?

hellog's

pops
were my favorite
      and the box was
      big and cheap
           so we got 'em
           often enough /

crisp
smacks against the tongue
      sweet something toof curling
      texture sent from heaven
           signed sealed delivered
           by coupons, clipped
                  with patience

goodstuff
bowls of the goodstuff /
      milky, crunchy, sugary goodstuff

pops
too common in the kitchen
      pop for my mouth,
      talkin too grown /
           talkin slick
           talkin back
                talkin troof
                talking in church
                    (even though that man
                      can get up there and run his mouf
                          and get applauded for it?
                          all my black ass got was

popped /
in the slope of the driveway
        by the hands of a styrofoam mother
        who feared the parts of her own creation
                which she could not claim as her own /

popped
for talkin like that
        for hanging with them
        for putting that status up on myspace
                with the words spelled like that
                for looking just like him in the face
                        laughing just like him /

pops
at breakfast when we had
        no time for a meal /
                pops
                for dinner when we smiled
                        through another 'breakfast for dinner'
                        pops when the leftovers stretched
                                inches beyond a plastic wallet's reach /

pops
on the way to wednesday night church
        and my arms remained crossed
        like that man hanging on that wall
                pops in a parking lot / pops when i was ungrateful
                pops, because i got em too and i turned out just
                fine
                        pops when all my darkest moments
                        were milky white
                                and all i could think about
                                was going to /

pop's,
who i'd see on the weekends

to atone for the stench
of colonizer fingerprints on me
    / pops, whose lips like thunder and lightning
    in the sky
    would sound the same way my lips sounded:
        rounded, full of clay, but with more
        bass,
            and everything i had to shed
            was embraced with ease, not /

pops
to teach the dog a lesson
    same one can't tell the difference
    between a tail and a chew toy
        supposed to learn something
        from /

pops
like dusty damn hand-me-downs
    that you stuck with
    cause you don't know no better
        and don't have the time right now
        to know no better cause you got
            a Black kid that's 16 years apart from you
            and two full time jobs and you're
            considering
                another / pops
                just like your mom before you
                    and hers before her and /

pops /
all the goodstuff
    all the goostuff all around
    even when pops wasn't around /
        pops / all the goodstuff all around
        all the time all the places / pops
            the easiest,

tax-free option
  the supper we slept to
  and rooster we woke to
      all the goodstuff
      pop / at new years for good
      luck
          because we don't have much
          time
          / pops /

because you're bowl's getting empty
pops / pops / pops
    that big yellow ass box
    i got tired of it / pops
        like it was that different
        than a whip
            pops like if i could do it all over again
            go back and pop right back / i would
                / pops / like i oughta sue
                hellog's
                    pops / like the word alone
                    makes my brain wanna go
                        pop

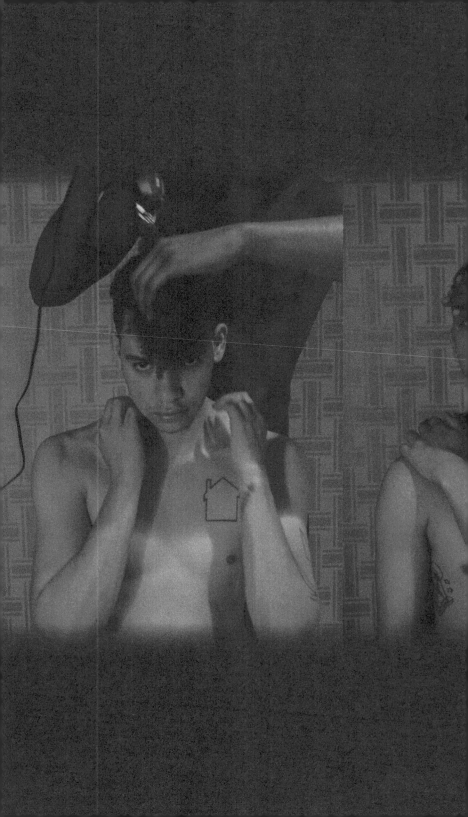

settlers, Atlanta, GA (May 2018)

a boot on my car, untameable time,
late for work, a bad fucking day.
outside my civic window, egg whites
canvassing at me with a clipboard.

> cauliflower in a khaki tone tells me
> to vote blue for black lives.
> teef talks about saving the future
> as if it's something we share.

> > printer paper in my face
> > waiting to be crumbled.
> > what's snow meant for
> > if not to be stepped on?

> > > porcelain squirms something serious
> > > when the response lets em know
> > > glasses of milk used to get spilled
> > > on these here sidewalks not long ago
> > > and maybe we should bring
> > > that back.

muslim niggas but the strap stays crossed.
might lose our minds but we never take a loss.
no sanctuary in the wild wild west
wipe the sweat from your neck
(when talking to ALLAH show respect)
atlanta boys came to jummah with a TEC
converted up norf, then brought it out west.
told him watch his neck, now he's praying fajr with a vest.

might have done it good but my niggas did it best.
(move more white than gentrification
move more black than gentrification
haram with the clip, total damnation
run up a check like sanctification
get it right back, accumulation
never worried about a reputation)

fuck your assimilation and white ass civilization
we move in unity like radical Haitians
we real cool like tropical vacations
pigs left a kufi crooked when bodies got wasted
now we bust back til someone's faceless
we the bomb, the blunt, the lost patience,

the dhikr, the prayer, fuck a federal agent,
tie an edgar and a hoover up in the basement,
we don't go to court, tooly makes the statement
talk to the feds and you can get faded
fuck your affiliation and the investigation,
fuck your arraignment fuck your temptation,
fuck your complacence and pig stations
fuck incarceration and your entire nation.

Beanie Sigel with a mic and bean pie
push a camel through a needle's eye,
we're the best that it gets. fuck your epithets
we're vicious, we're the end of the West.
nigga we are the threat. we are the threat.
grill bacon like we get waffle house checks.
put your dogs to sleep like we are the vet.
poke pork with a fork like it owes us a debt.
take the palms of their hands for our cigarettes.
agitate all three k's in amerika so it never forgets.
so it never forgets. my nigga, we are the threat.

my dad taught me
everything i know

and said that he would never ever
teach me everything he knows
and if i know one thing fasho
it's that if i don't escape
(by any means
whateverso)
i'm gonna
fucking
blow

tried to crawl underneath
saw no way to get over
couldn't get around
nothing left for me
to do but to go
straight thru
and burn it
all down

wallahi on everything—life,
(death even fucking closer)
if i don't make it out soon
then i ain't making it out
alive and there's no
seeking closure

i don't have to tell you what happened to
the landowners and dead sinners
who became beef stew
in habana when revolution flew:

bullets came thru and they knew
the bird had to bid the nest a quick adieu
because vengeance like rent became due

i promise i don't need no fuckin guidance
and anyways, it's not like you could provide it
but if i wake up tomorrow with the air still violent
i'm not going out silent, i'm pulling up with the violence
man this shit's about to blow, and it just can't decide when

what do you do when once again
the dopest dope still leaves you feeling hopeless hopes
and you don't drink don't smoke no smokeless smoke
way too close to being dead and broke to not chew
chew chew when they wanna see you choke
chopped and screwed, mad unprovoked
cough undiagnosed, life uneven yoked
death around on every fuckin corner
reminding you can get poked
just a few likkle keystrokes
away from your name
on an airbrush t-shirt
looking cheap and
tear-soaked

who teaches the wind to calm the fuck down for a second?
who teaches my eyes to keep looking straight ahead
when i drive by that tree that calls my damn name?
who teaches heartbeats to turn to weapons
when existence is again being threatened?

what can you take for the paranoia tremors at night?
who do you call for endless bleeding of the mind?
what do you do when there's no end in sight?
where do you hit if yourself you must fight?

who teaches the sky to cry and crack

and who taught me how to breathe?
i want a word with them
for what they did to me
and i want a word with my dad
for teaching me everything i know
and not teaching me everything he knows.

and once again i find myself here
at the place where the margins fold inward
returning to that same tenseness
that last time left my mental splintered
(and again it is now swelling within me
at what feels like an uncontrollable speed
like an engorged belly exploding,
or where a river turns to sea)

> *i cannot eat any more death--*
> *my jaw is sore my teef*
> *are breaking my ribs*
> *are bursting,*

                                        (help me, please)

it is my job to write. it is my job to write.
it is my job to right. it is my job name.
it is my job to dwell in chest-deep rages.
it is my job to free truths from their cages.
and it is, once again, my job to bleed
to create my self again from flesh unfreed
and remind again of the poplar trees
and the ropes swinging in the breeze
(and the bodies that still hang today
that haunt all of time and space)

of the corpses that could never decay

of the blood waiting in the doorway

of every home built on stolen land

the blood on every single pigs' hand

the names and faces of the damned

who will one day rise from the soil, sea and sand

by revolutionary means we may not yet understand.

everybody knows when i break

everybody knows when i ache

it's in everything i create, everything i write.

everybody knows when the waterfall dries

we gotta go back to the lake and revise.

i'm still learning to come up with a plan

to deal with it without revealing my hand

to get back to making without breaking

and smiling wide without faking.

i'm doing everything that i fucking can

but all's been damned since i went to mississippi[4],

GODDAM

---

4   Inspired by Nina Simone's stunning protest song "Mississippi Goddam," this poem was written while I was in Mississippi filming for the documentary "Parchman Prison: Pain & Protest." My first time in Mississippi, my time spent there was incredibly emotional, and it made me reflect deeply on my role as a journalist and documenter.

we've gotta bring back muthufucka
not "motherfucker!" or whatever
i mean *muthufucka*
like the repo muthufuckin man
like who is this muthufucka rollin' through my neighhood
like this muthufuckin cracker
we had to tear this muthufucka up
that muthufucka has my money
like the dj's playing my muthufuckin jam!
and it's time for you to shout your favorite part
like *get back muthafucka! you don't know me like that!*

i'm talking about the *muthufucka*
that carries the same energy as
butch queens slipping *bitch* out their moufs
when something tastes like oolong

like *run for cover muthufuckas*
like waiting on the muthufuckin train
like waiting on your late muthufuckin check
as in the white muthufuckas holding up your money again
and "black banks" can't do a muthufuckin thing about it
again
like we're higher than a muthufucka
like who is this muthufucka?
like these muthufuckin snakes
        on the muthufuckin plane
off with their muthufuckin heads
like make that muhufucka hammer time
'cause that's what a muthufuckin monster do,

MUTHUFUCKA!

the apocalypse[5]

---

was rhodesia was israel
was the united east india company
was new zealand and australia
was jim crow and jim jones
was human chattel and slave patrols
was the bureau of indian affairs,
millionaires and billionaires.
it was the six hundred and thirty-five thousand
tons of bomb and napalm dropped on korea
was the flavor-aid nine hundred and nine
people drank in the guyanese jungle
was the stripes on my ancestors' backs
was the stripes on your ancestors' backs
the cherrytree george washington never cut down
was protests turned photo ops
was marches turned magazine covers
was burning precincts turned representation
was the gap in madonna's teef
was the bullets in robert olsen's gun
was the smoke and rubble left at 6221 osage ave
was the wounds in Assata's back
was enemy of the sun found sitting in
George Jackson's cell after his murder.
the apocalypse was Marsha P. Johnson's body
found floating in the hudson river
was canada and was germany
was the dutch was the portuguese
was amerika's grip on Cuba and Venezuela and
Hawaii and Puerto Rico and Guam and
Iraq and Haiti and indian residential schools
was the miami gusanos cheering for Fidel's death
was Tony McDade's last breath
was Kalief Browder's last breath

5   Originally published in *Protean Magazine*, November 3, 2020.

was Sandra Bland's last breath
was Nat Turner's last breath
was Muhlaysia Booker's last breath
was Sankara's and Lumumba's last breaths
was Winnie and Mumia's prison cells
was the taste of blood filling Fred Hampton's mouth
before they dragged him into the hallways
and left him lying in a pool of blood.
the apocalypse was trump
was obama and biden and hillary and bernie
was eisenhower and carter and hoover and
cleveland and washington and taft and lincoln
was diamond, lithium, oil, cobalt, coltan,
gold, tungsten, and copper in the Congo,
was JUNE 13 1980 when gregory smith
gave Walter Rodney the walkie talkie,
was enslaved poems illegal to be written
was Harriet Powers' quilts
was Dave the Potter's encrypted messages
was the failure of the maji maji rebellion
was hijabs snatched and weddings bombed
was fourteen-year-old James Doxtator's remains never found
and you reading this poem not knowing his name
was fourteen-year-old Giovanni Melton
snatched from life and the world not caring
because no body ever cares
when you're young black gay and dead
was Human
was internment camps
was blackwater mercenaries
was mao's last poem
was Fanon's leukemia
was Bob Marley's melanoma
was Gamba Adisa's breast cancer
was Eleanor Bumpurs shotgunned
against her kitchen wall by rent marshalls
was the barracoon.
the apocalypse was already here,
it has been here, striking in plain sight,
it is not a thief in the night we must watch for

nor an impending catastrophe we must manage
but an infestation so large, so vast in sheer numbers,
so incalculable in the lives it's collected
and audacious in the histories its stolen,
that we think it has yet to arrive.

(the **weight**

of the apocalypse is heavy, and we all carry it even if we don't realize it.

We, as in butch queens, the gworls, creatures of the night, and shady theydies.

We, as in niggas, niggettes, and nigglets from Angola to Atlanna.

We, as in the wretched of the soil plucked pruned and sold at shop.

We, as in the tragic mulattxs struggling to pick a place on the same damn wall.

We, as in the muthufuckas on the other side of a pig's gun.

We, who buss back.

We, as in i was on free lunch and handmedowns and got bullied for that shit.

We, as in the meek struggling to inherit a doomed earth.

We, who were forced to make a home of the shadows when everything light tried to kill us.

We, who inhale sulfur and chew rust to pay for bread and milk.

We, who navigate blockades, apartheid walls, and ghetto birds to give birth.

We, who become acquainted with the quality of our own blood and call it survival.

We, who hear talk of ~~western~~ culture and with instinct pull out our knives—or at least make sure they're within reach.[6]

We, who carry the weight of the ocean, and the millions of apocalypses who chose waves when land was no longer an option, know the dents in our shoulders intimately.

We carry it with us daily.)

6   Frantz Fanon, *Wretched of the Earth*. "But it so happens that when the native hears a speech about Western culture he pulls out his knife—or at least he makes sure it is within reach."

for **Tort**—

a barrage of bullets,
someone died.
some protested,
others just cried.
cops did that thing
they always do
and lied.

a bacon cast iron in flames,
red ink sprayed against walls,
another hashtag added
to the symphony of names.
glass crunched under piggy boots
received more sympathy
than a defender of tree roots.

them piglets look us in the eyes
and speak claims of 'terror,'
while right here on peachtree
and auburn every night,
folks lay their tired heads
on cold sidewalks streets,
for them no tears nor fright.

a diaspora of pain
pushes a city to break
once again, and again,
and for those slain,
to the streets we take.

some protested,
others became untied.
a few even decided
it was finally time
to get unified.
cops did that thing
they always do
and lied.

dreaming of **days**

distant, cautiously captured in unrealized mediums
framed in unknown and terrifying futures
with an intrusive but welcome
calmness:

> sown pits and potted seeds will have burst
> through dirt in ritualistic dance,
> offering and relinquishing for years—
> trees growing for memories' sake
> and memories sake, only
> to litter the front yard just once more
> with fruit before the summer ends.

i look at every leaf and forever recollect
the rich taste of your lips with nectar all over them,
watching you stand beneath that tree and lick
your fingers like only i had ever seen you do,
the homes i made for you between the moon
and my embrace while these leaves watched.

> in the shade my children
> one day ask
> how we survived
> and i tell them
> we had no other options.

in the darkness my children
one day ask
about those
who did not survive
and generations of tears fall.

in the breeze my children
ask for that
banana pudding
i used to make for them
all the goodstuff that came with it
but the memory will no longer be
mine to keep safe and recreate.

in my home my children
one day ask
about the days
i could not breathe
and i will let them know
that to even be touched by
the breath of the Most High
was to know that my lungs
were no more mine than
the wind and the olive trees.

their children will find me some days
and walk me back inside from the tree.
home will be a old, tacky mesh of
earth, militant green, soft lavender, black bruises
and they will ask in giddy, kiddish tongues,
how we preserved. how we persevered.

never reserve truth from them—
as apokalyptic as it was
how we waded in unreality,
time bloomed burned and melted
before we chewed on it like taffy and snarled,
got cavities and truth aches
truth canals and fillings,
how we glyphos/ate dystopia for breakfast
scrolled thru coppercobaltaluminamironlithium coiled
blood diamonds for sport.

                    i'll let them know real estate agents,
                millionaires and landlords and cops
            (yes, the ones they heard of in those stories)
                and other criminals, crooked crackers,
                    politicians, and bounty hunters
                        all had reality shows
                    with dazzling production quality
                and budgets bigger than i'd ever know.

they will laugh and their friends may not believe
the ramblings of an old deaf beard and kufi
resting atop what's left of bone and pale skin.
so i'll press on:
we had movements that felt like life and death,
moments that felt like movements,
and life that didn't look much different
than death on most days.

we had to pay for everything
to everyone white and some of us even
ate roaches and took beatings and taunted death
on national fatback television screens
to pay for medical bills, college, groceries,
a home, attention.

i didn't walk to school in the snow for miles barefoot
but i damn sure did work my knees away
for them loans.

(when their minds wander
because their crazy grandparent
never learned to shut the hell up
and tells them same stories every time)
i'll let them know, too, about the days pulsing with heat
the lush of nature and natural laughter in our hair
pillows of smoke and greens on baltimore grass,
how we passed and puffed like it would be our last
the way we loved loudly with tension and energy,
shared poems worried together and ate fruit
stared apokalypse in the face another muthufuckin time
and took lovely little pictures by the rocks
grounded, or how sometimes after a few hours together
the world didn't feel like it was poisoning us,
like time wasn't in the air at alarming rates.

i will let them know that friendship sustained me
carried me and us, friends
who nurtured for a season before leaving
those who stayed thru the fire
or rinsed away in ash
and those who brought trouble as well.
how i knew my right hand less than
some comrades to my left
how we could look around
and see death stalking all of us.
the bombs that did not go off
the bullets that bounced off bones
the shattered teeth, bloody eyes,
bruised minds, tired spines,
the wounds we could not fix
the gashes we could not mend
the cuts we could not repair
the lives we could not salvage,
the breaths stolen in the dead of night
that i could never get back
the carnage:
handfuls of flesh and chained wrists
pools of deep red and black blood
we waded through until it all became normal,
the last kiss i gave a dead lover
before throwing my bricks.

                    humans incarcerated nature,
        i will say with smoke pouring from my nose
              and they will look dazed in confusion.
                       how else do you explain
                       the veins of our existence
                   imposing on the earth all around?
          i'll point to the sidewalk, the powerlines,
               the park where a parking lot used to be,
              the strips of green between airport runway
             where they now barefoot kick soccer balls
                   the dumpsters of beheaded flowers
                the rails we hold onto as we cross our paths
                  the leash folks walked their dogs on
                  the fences erected for their own sake
                      and the violence they maintained.
                          nature, too, was imprisoned.

when the candy of innocence wears off
and i'm told the children must rest their eyes
i will wrap them in love
and hold them there for a few moments.
silence. nothing but the sound of breathing.
nothing but the exuberance of quiet rest
and potential energy will exist in the doorway.

                      i will shed warm, gratified tears,
                     knowing the blood of my youth
                    sweat of my life and pain of struggle
                          was for nothing at all
                          if not for this child's peace,
         to see them baked in protection and horizons,
                       wrapped in unfamiliar calmness,
             choking on no peach pits nor on time,
         wholly acquainted with the patient goodstuff
         which i was never able to know or hold on to.

in the final moments before my eyes close,
again dreaming of days unfamiliar
when my lungs were weak
blood boiled like peanuts
apokalypse as routine,
them days still distant
more than the dreams
in the eyes of the youth,
i will calmly welcome the idea
that nothing was done in vain.

no more starvin for affection

from niggas
that wouldn't feed me
even if they could
no more lettin the lavender lullabies
sleep me thru fajr
no more missed prayers
no more puttin deja vu under my tongue
and trippin on yesterdays
no more chewin on thorns
but callin it planting roses
cause shit gets red either way

no more breakin blood
and callin it poetry
no more tirin two thumbs
and callin it revolutionary
no more runnin from lemon juice in wounds
no more lettin wounds fester neglected
no more believin the wolves
are licking the wound
to help heal it
when i can see flesh in their teef
no more wounds

no more suffocatin on the unsaid
no more fear of what's said
no more startin over
when persistence
is the harder choice
no more pushin thru
when rest is the harder choice
(no more hands on my body

that don't touch my soul)
no more free work no more free work
no more budgets
no more pickle juice
no more daggers no more grinnin
and no more bearin it
no more of what i deserve tasting like guilt
when it should feel like gold
no more analyzin and criticizin and problematizin
and theorizin for the sake of hearin my own voice

no more excess
no more handshakes
no more fucking zoom calls
no more "baby imma do right this time"
no more, baby. i'm so damn tired.
no more

RE/SOLUTIONS

don't wake **me** up

when i sleep
it's like tomorrow came
and passed me by
and i didn't care to notice

when i say
don't wake me up
unless it's an emergency,
me dying don't count.

when i snore
it's in spite of my boss
and my boss's boss
and the big boss too

so don't wake me up
til Mao wakes back up
and sends over the ammunition,
til the Pan-African Liberation Forces
are ready to takeover washington

don't wake me up
til that homeless person

pissin on lincoln's monument
has a bed to lay in at night
and he's totin a 45
in the people's liberation army

i'm not just restin my eyes
this time i'm fucking sleeping,
so don't touch the fucking remote
unless k!ng's out the pin
and the klintons are in the bin.

you think i can afford rest?
in this here dying economy?
whatever sleep you see me steal
was won with enough blood
to cover every doorframe in egypt,
so don't wake me before tomorrow does.

times are getting rough and my callouses are getting tough
and i don't know if this month the freelance shit will be
enough

      so puff puff muthufuckin pass before this blunt
      becomes our last
      before we have enough time to realize they're right on
      our ass

            you hear them drones hovering over the grass?
            they're coming fast
            so baby let's have a baby before biden does
            something crazy

                  let's have the niqah in the neighbor's
                  backyard real quick
                  then we gotta split, i think i heard 'em
                  pull up with a stick

fuck it baby let's get married right here in our yard where it's
shady
you been a lover a partner sometimes a nuisance sometimes a
friend

>> but more than anything a comrade and you're that til the
>> very end
>>> whether we go out with a pool of blood on the
>>> floor where we pray

>>> or in clothes with dirt stains or shotup in the
>>> driveway trying to get away
>>> i think it's safe to say they've got us either way
>>> so whatever comes our way

>>>> our only choice is to just say fuck it
>>>> let's have baby, baby
>>>> before they torture us until we go
>>>> batshit crazy

until the truth becomes hazy and our eyes become lazy
and we can't open them anymore, fuck it baby let's—[7]

7   Inspired by the title of the song, "BabyLet'sHaveaBabyBeforeBushDo-
Somethin'Crazy," by The Coup.

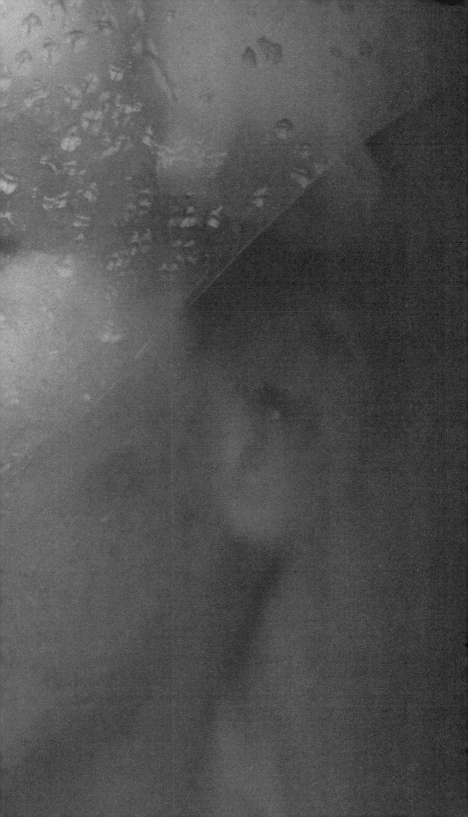

one **eye** open

two more closed /
put this on the back cover of my memoirs
that yall publish after i'm dead,
when folk talk about my influence
the same way they could have when i was alive.
use these words for my posthumous awards please /
while i'm in jannah watching clowns claim me.
when assholes publish my journals and unfinished sketches
without my consent / like they did with Basquiat and Van
Gogh
and Kahlo / put this poem on the back cover
and call it a cold day in hell.
when the cadillactivists come and go
crash their films sets and red carpets
throwing red paint on their blue vests,
don't let them know peace in life
if i can't meet peace in death
don't let me pay their bills / with death /
if i couldn't pay my rent while alive.
when yall put me on the shelf in the bookstore
next to killary and koates
or some other liberal i hated
and sh**n king writes my eulogy,
remember me as a pretty bitter nigga
who wanted to burn it all down.

when the riots arrive and the fires start,
my white mother may go on cnn or msnbc or
one of those news channels / i spent careers hating /
and speak of peaceful protests in my name:

you have my permission to remind her
that the child she gave and lost
was prepared to give and lose it all
and would do it all again should the chance arise /
so the word 'peaceful' doesn't need to come from her lips.
one eye open, two more closed.
if they put my face on a t-shirt
make sure it's airbrushed,
cut it into a crop top and wear it to a protest.
let the dudes who set up tables and sell shirts
outside of the metro stations make a good
profit from me / until the next person
needs to be screenprinted and sold.
send a few shirts to trump and to obama,
i was always sure they had similar taste.
please don't let them think-piece me, goddammit.

my hair was my prized possession,
so burn that on the steps of the whiteness house
and tell them thanks for the ride
or bottle it and ship it to someone who cares.
at my memorial when people cry in pain for me
more than they made eye contact with me / in life
charge them by the minute. tell them they can
purchase video if they want to add it to their reels.
use the money to buy my mom a book on revolution,
get justin, cj, and avery some new shoes,
and buy carlos that helmet case he always wanted
before it's time to put me in the ground.
when they throw dirt on my name
plant a damn seed, grow some lavender,
and keep shit moving.

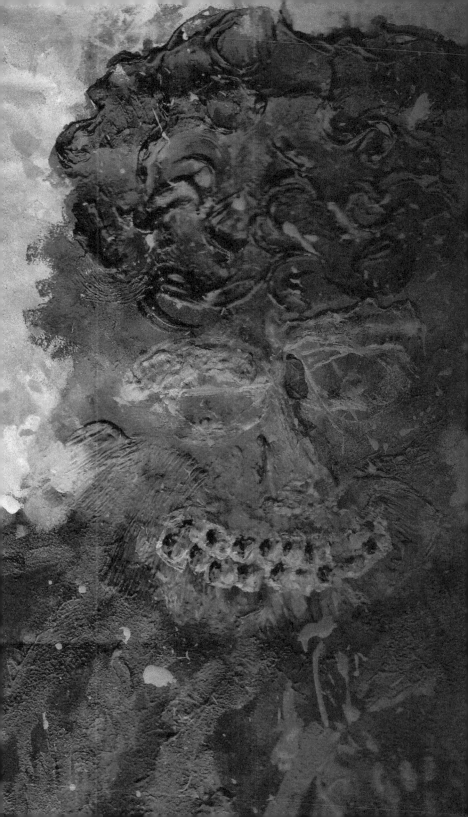

2

"endure patiently what befalls you /
surely this is a resolve to aspire to"

everybody talks about wanting a plate
until it's time to pick up the fork and fucking eat

if you say you want to kill me
i respect it more if you mean it

if you hit me you better kill me
because when it's my turn
i'm not hesitating nor missing

if you say you want to hurt me
i'll take it more seriously if you do

if grief is proof of love
then this rage is proof of existence

life is proof of death
and cigarettes are evidence for satisfaction

imagine, someone tries to rob your home
but just roasts you for having ugly shit

because you thought if you could afford to buy it
then it must look nice

you aspire to a resolve you'll never achieve because you're
addicted to stimulation and speak like the braying of a
donkey.

obsessive note #22

what happens if i tell (You) how paranoid i really am?
if i say aloud that i'm fucking terrified of the dunya's shadow
and standing on uneven ice is growing exhausting?
what happens when i can't outgrow the feeling?
       that i lock my doors in multiples of fours
       but i ain't *crazy enough* to tell folks.

no matter how empowered the .45 makes me feel
or how safe the security system pretends to be
there's still a sticky paranoia underneath my heel.
like if i didn't cook it then i don't want to eat the meal,
to sleep i need something way stronger than chamomile.

when do they start worrying? when do they lock me away?
how much worse can it get, how much of insanity's foreplay?
losing weight, pacing, breaking, gripping,
questioning myself steadily,

desperately seeking clarity.
is there a line
and if so
have i crossed it already?

i **scare** myself

some times
leaning
too close
to the blade
of my own heartbeat.

trembling
my bones
as they realize
the bass of that
wheezy organ
thumping away.

i can't think and breath
at the same time some times
when the nebula of thoughts
is too heavy on my neck.

how the fuck else
do i say this,
if not in poetry:

some times
suffering
too close
to the surface
of life's window
trembles your foundation,
until you begin sinking fast
waste-deep into capitalism's
deadly old colonial quicksand

struggling just to get out the landfill.

i used to share carelessly
about the shadowy doubts
i battled, but this shit right here?
beastly unlike anything i've tamed.

i'm supposed to pay $50 for a session
magically find $125 to see the psych
(7 minutes 13 seconds on the dot)
another $210 for the meds
do it all again next month
and the next after that
when i can just write
this poem right here
free of charge?

some times i strike fear into my own gut
scared about that cloud on the head
churning out thought after thought after
thought, intrusive, endlessly supplied.

(why can i only tell You about this in **poetry** and **prayer**?
why do the words come out so difficult in speech,
but smooth on the page?
what are You trying to teach me
        by taking away my lips,
        my mouf, my **voice**,
hurdling my thoughts?)

ontological dust,
or their **overall** uselessness

they dream of dust.
dying in life
for a taste of
                dust.

cups filled with despair
that will make them want
to focus the rest of their lives
on getting more
                despair.

pages of poetry knowing no reason
for existence beyond the
                page.

sharp forks of representatives
shoved down the throats of gulls
until the metal pokes through skin
                (again).

i knew decay had death for me
the same week i salvaged the bones
and had nothing to show for it but more
                death.

we all knew the fucking heat death had for us
in the very moment we carnaged the body
and had nothing to show for it but more
                heat.

days where the blessing
is that it just fucking
hurts.

they dreamt of dust
and instead got
ashes.

they asked for crumbs
and instead got
ants.

they looked towards the ground
and missed warning of the
rain.

they set their sights on dead days
and so they became
lifeless.

we chewed on mustard seeds
and shared sweet dates
until dreams surpassed
sand.

we died in the name of deliverance
and emancipation grew from the
dirt.

we gave ourselves over to the night
and from it birthed jet black new
life.

(the angels couldn't get god
        to order them a taxi in time.
                said they couldn't get to me
                        sanctions—oil shortage in heaven.

demons ran so muthuhfuckin fast,
        i got away for a little while but
                all my years of track and field
                        didn't prepare me for that race.

i told the mirror if i failed a third time
        then i wouldn't tell a single soul.
                and if i succeeded i would tell
                        everyone—simple math.

felt like the moment when a character
        stares directly into the glassy camera,
                realizes that their next move will
                        alter the entire trajectory of their life.

then the dream ends.
        a consistent failure, per usual.
                a mouthful of dusty disaster
                        losing to life once again.)

(i suffered quietly like i was told to do.

i suffered loudly—they said it would feel good. i suffered in words, in photographs, on and off cameras.
i suffered alone and in groups, in the underground among harsh whispers and flaccid truths,
surrounded by people i love, some who wanted to kill me. others who merely held me while i birthed sorrow.
i suffered enough for handfuls of tomorrows and i suffered enough to put yesterdays to shame.

i suffered in face masks, bubble baths, and on planes. i suffered with my passport in hand
and i suffered in a kitchen full of comfort food. in poverty. in black and, unfortunately, in white.
i suffered enough to share with an entire village. nervously, out of the way. on display. ambiguously.

no matter how i do it, even when quietly, alone in a corner, away from the world, it's never enough.
i never run out of suffering and it never runs out of me.)

title somewhere under my african authoritarian **communist** boot

I am nonchalant to the bullshit! (Yeah)
Yes, all of my thoughts are intrusive!
             [...]
                    I'm only here to smoke more blunts,
                    And spit on racist cunts!
                              —RICO NASTY, "INTRUSIVE"

everywhere disorder and confusion!
it's a jungle out here, have no delusions!
word to the Mr. Monk theme music!
a jungle out there, said Randy Newman!
the jungle's in my head and it's protrudin!
yes, all of my thoughts are intrusive!
my last asthma attack was abusive!
i like to live my life very reclusive!
i dream of pulling triggers over bullshit!
so don't make me do it!

my thoughts might drown me
in the deep end!!
they like to grab my ankles
when i'm sinkin!!
i'm your favorite writer's favorite writer,
i know you peep'd it!
garden full of snakes, cut the grass,
i grim reap'd it!!
all that fake love,
yall can keep it!!!!
i'll keep talking to my self
before i entertain a weak bitch!
discipline saved me
now i really don't see shit!
you bitches really suck,
yes yall can eat shit!
if you see a crow one day
then think of me and eat it!!

fuck your bullshit sophistication!
i'm not here for academic patience!
you bitches need an authoritarian vacation!
i'll stomp your degrees and education!
make a bonfire from all your publications!

I wish death on all of you bitches.
—RICO NASTY, "SWAMP BITCHES"

seen

the snap of a camera
clicks in the distance,
but i'm too busy
to notice.

spent too much time
searching for mirrors
and calling it love,
so now when a mirror looks at me
i can't make sense of what i'm seeing.

i remember when i had to be in class by 8am,
clocked in at my day job at 3pm,
the night job around 11pm,
organizing every weekend,
nothing in between but crinkly dollars,
handfuls of dreary dreams, bad friends,
and a nap in the back of a 96 honda civic.

i had days that fully convinced me
i wasn't supposed to see the night,
nights where i would have lost myself
in another mirror if i hadn't seen the light.

to be seen was a lilac wrapped dream,
believed eyes on me was a need,
even when the sharp snips of attention
pushed me towards busting at the seems.

years later smoking in a room of love
i got asked by a kind stranger
why i was more of an observer,
a listener, a fly on all walls
no longer needing to be seen
but addicted to seeing:

the cost of being seen
is invisibility, funny as it is.
seen until see-through.
until the mirrors crack
and 10 years bad luck ensues.
speak. write. think. run. jump. do.
them years in the grind
all leave people's minds,
eventually, you ain't nothing
but an object in blue.

you'd get tired of being seen, too.

it's getting bad again.
and i don't know why
       or how to explain it but i feel my self
       falling from the edges once more.
       i ran from it for years and was successful
       until my heels wore to the bone: 96 honda crashed

       i always feel cut down in the winter
but this time ALLAH pulled up my roots
       and that other other kind of cold set in,
       bled into spring, and i felt the worst nearby.

       i was supposed to be iron. i didn't notice the signs /
and it damn near left me for dead on a d.c. bench
       with no time to save my self / for me to
       step in when i could have quelled the pain.
       now i wait by the phone. avoid clutter. i pray
       and cherish your voice. hold polaroids tight.

       plant when i cannot harvest,
gasping for air, or begging for a slice of silence,
       whichever fucking comes first.
       the compulsions return, i know
       they're here to stay—

IT'S GETTING BAD AGAIN

lumpenproletariat **blues** for MonteQarlo's platinum blonde wig[8]

> He *loudly proclaims that he has nothing to do with these Mau-Mau,*
> *these terrorists, these throat-slitters.*
> —FRANTZ FANON, THE WRETCHED OF THE EARTH,
> "CONCERNING VIOLENCE"

(i've known ghosts and ghouls who walk like heaven depends on it; pot holes deep enough to admit they want to ruin those who pass over them; grains of sand strong enough to acknowledge how unlikely it is to become glass. we bonded over roads diverged apokalyptic pasts and seeing everything in red.

the last true drag queen i knew was a bad bitch that could swish pepperspray like listerine and always heard her music playing on chevy radios in heaven when others couldn't hear it /

inna lillahi wa inna ilayhi raji'un. i found my way to where the smell of her incense runs away and left bundles of roses, lavender, plums, saffron, and gold for her to carry with her.

weirdos kept me sharp and safe when the textbooks dulled my edge, and the closest i've gotten to god was when she asked if she could bum a cigarette with her hand already stretched out towards me. she knew death and rocky horror and didn't give a single fuck if i thought she looked greedy. she told me so much

8   First published in *Protean Magazine*, 2023.

about life, i ended up learning about death.

she showed me nights where the air feels crowded[9] and triggers aren't pulled yet bones somewhere crack all the same. first time a shadow realizes Fanon ain't talkin' butter knives: same night a blade itches to press against the musty neck of a colonizer.

i've heard stories of sheiks who put down the good book and picked up a piece of metal when time came. i've watched clowns and carnies throw stronger punches than those creeps in suits and ties who wear masks in layers, and i've seen high-heeled jokes snuff a crinkled sheet of porcelaine paper from underneath thirty six inches of platinum blonde synthetic with ease.)

9   Listen in on SoundCloud: https://soundcloud.com/monteqarlo/world-is-crowded

(i forgot to **breathe**.

i lost my breath
and begging ev
trying to talk thr
through the par
weathering eve

ming and yelling
e else to **inhale**
ne tears and work
and all the fears
m in every wind

anwhile, I **gasped** for air.)

the breaths that i steal /

waking up feels surreal /

especially when dying /

keep it real i'd be lying /

when only dead bodies /

cause who protects me /

who stops the bullet /

who turns the knife /

who asks where i been /

and wipes blood off my chin /

~~but hey, maybe I'll never win /~~

~~can't let the devil in /~~

but when the wind blows /

i'm wasting no time /

depend on heaven's mercy /

and the blessings are blurry /

feels like less controversy /

if i said the shit don't hurt me /

seem to be protest worthy /

when me and death are flirting? /

if the blood's already squirting? /

when no one's observing? /

when the paranoia sets in /

when i lose my mind again? /

~~maybe I'm settlin /~~

~~I'm a comic book heroine /~~

make no comparisons /

going out like a

SUICIDE VETERAN

i breathe often. (but never enough.)
gold curled all in my hair—
waiting to be cut but knowing
i am not eager to pawn it,
armed with shadows of doubt
that fall over contours of sorrow
like the stripes on my backside.
i breathe often. (but never enough.)

stench

i rinse myself five times daily
intentions pure pouring water
from my hands over my face,
yet the stench never evades me.

my therapist always jokingly says
showers are a big problem for me
but i see nothing so wrong anyways
spending an hour or two scrubbing.

in the sun i embrace the burning,
hope the scent is singed from my skin.
nature doesn't have to dig deep within
to hear these thoughts squirming.

cast my face towards the earth,
a hundred brothers in the room
all facing precisely eastward:
anxious, i wonder if they can smell it too.

the days when the imam comes down from the pulpit,
crosses his thobed legs atop one another,
gives the khutbah from the floor at eye level,
terrify me, because i wonder if he'll catch a whiff.

i remember 14, leaning out the bedroom window
my arm perched on a sill, knees on a chair,
sneaking sips of cigarettes thinking i was so clever,
as if the smell didn't latch onto my clothes.

toothpaste stuck on the corners of my lips,
i scrub something furious and brutal
trying to make my breath please my chin,
and yet still, all attempts remain futile.

if i can smell it, they probably can too.
consciousness of the Self, a worldly thing.
drown me in sanitizer, i don't care if it stings.
when that don't work neither, what am i to do?

in the same fashion i wear strong cologne,
roll oils on my wrists, keep my neck sweet,
all in hopes that when i hug my Maker
he doesn't smell the dunya on me.

curb meet **stomp**

And then they come out like roaches
p-p-pecking away like vultures.
—Nicki Minaj, "Last Chance"

if you stare too hard you'll see the rats
the roaches the ants in all the cracks

look too long you'll see the bony little tails
and tiny nails scattering along without fail

mister officer, i don't gotta own this car to fuck in it
ya Allah, i run from the dunya with a foot stuck in it

if you stare too long you'll see the rats
and knowing they're there will ruin your day

i don't know why the piggy had his head in the way
who told his neck spleen and face to take that bullet?

get too lost in your thoughts lose your head
take too long to answer wind up dead

hit the blunt too hard you'll see The Creator
miss too many court dates see the undertaker

say the wrong thing and lose all your paper
let your guard down prepare to meet your Maker

if you stare just enough you can see the rats
running back and forth on their little tracks

running underneath drive thru car wheels

fighting off all them dangerous alley cats

scuse me sir, i was getting my dick sucked in that seat
a whole metro here why the fuck you gotta sit near me?

them rats pray to the same god as me
whether they fucking realize it or not

if you stare with your good eye you'll see the rats
and spend a good while wishing you didn't

(leave my vicinity with their head dented
don't talk about it but really did it)

raised my voice at THE MERCIFUL got my throat slashed
talked down to myself got my shit mashed

hit me with that taser little piggy i need to feel something
put me down great Ar-Raheem show no mercy

i looked too closely. saw the rats.
and in this world you can't unsee that

(when you're done apologizing to the emotions you've silenced:
find me. when you're done running your blood through coffee filters:
find me. when you're finished prosecuting dead air: find me.)

ocd **vlog** #7

my adhan rings from the creases of my palm now,
startles the part of my self baffled by peace
corporate ads intrude across the quran app
/ digital divinity asks for a subscription price

notifications fall from the top of the screen
when i watch the weekly jummah livestream,
anxiety pushes my breathing beyond its limits
when i throw my face into buzzing masses

i speak to YOU / between a raging sea
and the peaceful quiet of your nearness
i rinsed skin wet something obsessive to get here
embraced whispers of ancestors against my cheeks

intrusive is the shadowy stench of the dunya
washed, spiraled down the drain
as i arrange myself to face YOU
dhuhr interrupted by the inescapable heartbeat

/ an inimitable worry within every breathe
damn near dead from the compulsions,
intrusive is the anvil above me

with its breathtaking weight

(and somehow, each time without fail
You lift that weight with such ease
cast doubt that it was ever even there
hold me tightly clutched at the heel)

stammered breathing, botched heartbeat
melt into the sea of prayer around me,
unmoored by the room's determination to You:
free cognitive behavioral therapy five times a day.

smokin **roaches**

how you know you gotta problem

    smokin roaches

look on yo face is so damn solemn

    smokin roaches

filter to the back of the throat,
parsin through the ashtray
saddest troof i ever wrote

    smokin roaches

convincin myself that the scraps
are sumthin more than leftovers

    smokin roaches

and just maybe perhaps
this lil bit will help me get over

    smokin roaches

even tho i know that dope equals death,
still out here pinchin pennies for grams
knowing it could be my last breath

    smokin roaches

i know what it does to my head,

know it brings me one step closer
to agents of the state
hitting me with that infrared

    smokin roaches

including those who deserve it,
makin body bags outta alphabet boys
tell em all to 5 times observe it

    smokin roaches

that's how i know i gotta problem

i shot **myself** with a sawed off

in the chest
in a dream
last night
and died.

in my nightmares,
i always survive.

let me make **one** thing clear

: they do not leave

they may be shushed
down to a mum hum
but they do not leave

they may argue violently
among each other endlessly
but never walk away /

matches under my ear
hanging from my eyelids
but they're never gone

they ask for fours
they demand, not ask
i count in fours

and when i don't give it to them
they eat at my lungs
until i just concede
and give them four

they don't leave, ever
bedbugs on a mission
fleas with a plan

lock the door again
it didn't feel right
do it again, now

listen for the death,
it's coming around soon
you know it's true

breath wrong and die
again and again and
again and again, death

hefty doses of lexapro

and lamictal and trazodone
only maim, never kill.

i have watched them
spoken with true ferocity
as they swing and
swing and swing and
swing from one side
to another, and another
and still never leaving /

they have chilled me
into choosing death
when i chose
threes over fours /
they have tasked me
onto anxious ledges
for daring to breath
out of line /
and have forced me
to add slanted lines
to the stanzas /
which break the pattern

i expect no understanding
delivered from any body
who still patiently waits
for the voices' departure

they never, ever do.
no suffocation ends them
no compulsion pleases them
no magic prays them
no dream unbirths them
while they nightmare you.

they wade into conversations
uninvited, always, of course
demanding an attentive audience.
they never, ever leave.

HELP! i accidentally told **my** therapist too much and now she wants to lock **me** up!

and if i'm going out
best believe
it will be on
my own fucking terms

> and if i'm down that bad
> for long enough
> just put me
> six feet under

> > and when the bullets fly
> > don't say i didn't warn you
> > or that fucking flag outside
> > what it was gonna to come to

> > > and when the anger
> > > has nowhere left to hide
> > > it'll turn inward on me
> > > and eat me from the inside

i'll cut my wrists and die
before i let some foul shit slide
before i let the pigs do it
i'll grab the handle and drive

> lexapro and lamictal won't stop
> them drones overhead
> risperidone ain't done a damn thing

for the voices in my head

      it's a compulsion
      if i scrub my hands
      but it's casual politics
      when they shot my mans

        it's a crime
        when i sell grams
        but business as usual
        when they draw prison plans

i'd rather slit my wrists than check myself in
    and just to be real fucking clear:
        you can gon ahead and send them pigs
           but i'll be dead by the time they get
           here

#233

these drafts rarely make it
past my fingertips

i suck my digits
until i taste bone

spit the words from my lips
marrow onto paper

> broth of emotion and salt
> salve for sadness in the throat

from experience i stumble
unsure of past and future alike

phrases fumble, feet unstable
as i try to put into lyric:

the touch of your madness
slices of softness against me

> i wade in troubled words, waters, and thoughts
> struggling to capture the prayer of YOUR beauty

insomnia note #3—6:15am

dear friend,
i've fallen in love
with the dark dirty dismal
corners of the nighttime

the moon's underbelly is warm
pulsing with dreary life
shaking in unease and hindsight

i grew accustomed to colorful calamity
crashed pasts and car wrecks,
something about the blood
brought me some sanity

my eyes laminated
to the corners of motel lots
workers turning dollars to cigarettes
learned me by name

when sleep antagonizes me,
i get my ass up and out
and into trouble:

traded death with a dealer in an econo-lodge
dealt favors for a muslim one floor up
saw a back blown out with the door wide open
watched someone get robbed in the lot
barely made it out alive too many times

the night is the bottom of a serpent
with the gloss of fresh death against it,
when you let the night lead
you never stop moving

i can't tell you how many times
my fight or flight kicked in
and i just had to see it through

how many nights fear kept me alive
up close and always personal with doom
the way i foam at the mouth something obsessive
for a slice of excitement should be outlawed

staying up like this
waiting for the night
to run into the sunrise
should be illegal

insomnia **note** #6—4:27am

dear friend,
i saw another crash tonight
you were the first person
i thought to tell
because when i called you
that one time i crashed
you were the only one
who didn't tell me to go to hell

there was fire coming from the hood
with thick red liquid dripping from a forehead,
another holding the bottom of their back in pain
and someone else frantically on their cell

i walked over to ask them if they were ok
and they didn't know what to say,
i offered support until help arrived
but they seemed offended by the gesture
like they was too scared
as to why i was up and out on foot
at this time of the nightmorning
to dare accept any solace from me

the look on their faces frightened me, too

insomnia note #17—3:45am

dear friend,
last night i watch a knife
slice a flesh wound
into the edges
of a black man's ribs

it felt so surreal
like watching adam
trying to snatch
his rib back

i laughed on accident
when my therapist told me
insomnia can be deadly:
it hurts your brain
stresses your heart
forces them to work overtime
can progressively get worse
until your mental deteriorates

everything moved in lackluster motion
when he pulled the blade from his jacket
a flash of rusty silver and black plastic
captivated all attention in a split second
war of words turned to blood soaked blows

if it wasn't for insomnia
i wouldn't be here
in this situation
in this parking lot

with a piece of gravel
lodged in my slides

i wouldn't be a witness
to the crimes of the night
nor on the edge of life
every time i get the chance,
maybe that's what
makes it so deadly

insomnia **note** #33 — 5:13am

dear friend,
there's a point in each night
when the moon sloppy kisses the earth
that few people are lucky enough to know

the sky a bright blackish purple
wrapped in peaceful silence
as it prostrates to make salat
before the morning comes

i buzz around the neighborhood
basking in its moonful glory
quiet feelings fall on a loud mind
few cars pass by, streets clear

the rush of a train persists in the distance
a cat races into the stealth of the shadows
trees present themselves in new form
death quiets its whispers in my ear for a moment

fleeting, this moment always already too short
silence disrupted by early morning commuters
the loud crash of a sunrise above barking dogs
as the moon loosens its lips from the earth

if i could marry these moments, i'd be the bride
if i could swallow the silence whole, i would gulp
if they could hook an IV bag up to my arms
and inject me with this peace, i'd rush to the ER

insomnia note #34 — 4:05am

dear friend,
tonight i realized
something i already knew:

the highs all eventually dull
with age and experience,
but the lows
can always
dig lower

talk is **clutter**

---

is the stumble from hoarded boxes blocking pathways,
is dusty knicknacks, small glass things no one needs
ornamental plastics, collected commodities clumsily displayed,

piles of news and papers collecting dust on shelves,
is cheap clothes fallen from hangers, scents unidentifiable,
is items lost and hiding and found unopened.

action is a silent thing that heals wholly.
silence is an active thing that can fold,
that can hold, that can bring sage
to rooms in desperate need of cleansing
and clear paths for itself. is a lavender calm
that's as angry as it is tearful. is a prayer rug.
and i am so tired of the clutter.

re:birth

i am not transforming into
a new or better person,
my eyes are not birthing
new nor unseen life.

i am simply healing back to
who i am supposed to be.
and maybe that process
looks to you like renewal

rather than a return to the source
in the truest sense of the phrase,
but let me assure you
i'm healing all the same.

i'm healing all the same.

after**word**

in the most consequential sense possible, i haven't spoken to the world in a while. i've written tweets here and there, maintained a steady stream of writing on my blog, published a few articles, spoken at protests and conferences, had my name appear in some peer-reviewed journals, recorded some podcasts, sat on a couple livestreams. but creating content, it must be said, is not the same as speaking to the world.

i have not stared the earth in its stunning face and spoken directly to it in many years. the last time i did so was *Grayish-Black*, when everything from organizing, mental illness, and identities were somewhat new to me; that book was an attempt at something i'd only realize within shuddering moments of embarrassment rereading it for the first time years later. in truth, i'm proud of the person i was when i wrote that collection, but earnestly recognize that *he* is dead and gone, and not coming back.

a lot has changed since the last time i had something to say. i almost died a few times, my anxieties developed anxieties, i touched a battlefield of sorts, and ultimately got scarred watching a lot burn down. friendships—which i would have bet my life on at one point—suddenly singed away to ashes from flames; revolution came and didn't happen right in front of my face; i watched book deals, recognition, speaking gigs, podcasts, dope, and, at times, mere pats on the back buy off an entire generation of would-be organizers; decades of counter-insurgency has made itself as ubiquitous as the glyphosate in our morning oats. i lost more friends, family, and comrades in the last few years than i could count on my hands, and everything just kept moving so quickly. i got trapped in a saga of some of the worst, most exploitative, racist workplaces i've ever experienced in my life—from so-called communists, too.

even more pressing and present this time around, i suffered health crises—some serious shit that shook me down to my core. there were weeks where i couldn't leave my room, moments when i wanted to try to end it all once again, and days that stretched for years. in an alexandria emergency room, i thought they were going to let me die on that hospital bed; they left trash lying on top of me, my arms poked and prodded in every direction and unable to move the shit off me; they forced me to pee in a bottle in a public room, despite me telling them i'm Muslim and it's important that i have privacy, all because they were *certain* i was on drugs; i overheard the nurses whispering laughter at my pain. just a week prior on a bench in gravely park, a homeless man with a beautiful smile and soft hands saved my life. i'm still trying to make sense of it all, and am grateful that i had the discernment not to live-tweet my pain and signal to the hyenas that i was wounded.

i'm not sure how much of this note is making sense to you, the reader, or not, but that is also part of the problem: you go through enough mental breakdowns, fight enough futile battles, give too much of yourself in the name of organizing for a stunted revolution, and your brain don't work the same way no more. i don't think the way i once did, and i can't speak the good word like i used to, and it's a challenge to write like i used to. my mind stutters. it's littered at times with intrusive thoughts, bloody doubt, and morbid paranoia. i used to form sentences worthy of gold, now sometimes i struggle to form words worth a lump of coal. so is life.

times is changing and i am too, and it is this reality which lends itself so graciously to poetry. i write poetry, so much poetry, every single day through muscle memory without fail, because if the vinyl of my thoughts scratch, it's simply an excuse to go to the next line. there is something i am afforded in poetry, being prepared to kill myself, as Lorde once said, and it feels sublime. the poems in this collection date mostly between 2019 to early 2023, and they tell stories and observations and thoughts and experiences that i don't know how else i would express if not through the power of the poem.

any mistakes or future self-embarrassments found henceforth, then, are all my own, and are in no way a reflection of The Most High whose perfection has guided me through the worst times imaginable. and should a single line in any piece of poem touch you, that too is but a reflection of The Most High's imprint on me.

enjoy.

—D. Musa Springer
2023

Printed in the USA
CPSIA information can be obtained
at www.ICGtesting.com
JSHW021919180824
68357JS00003B/13

9 781088 025673